MW00872918

Summer on the Farm

Elva Hurst

HARVEST HOUSE PUBLISHERS
EUGENE, OREGON

Cover by Aesthetic Soup, Shakoppe, Minnesota

SUMMER ON THE FARM
Copyright © 2014 by Elva Hurst; Illustrations by Elva Hurst
Published by Harvest House Publishers
Eugene, Oregon 97402
www.harvesthousepublishers.com

Library of Congress Cataloging-in-Publication Data
  Hurst, Elva, 1968-
  Summer on the farm / Elva Hurst.
      pages cm – – (Farm life series)
  Summary: Eleven-year-old Elva has a very busy summer splash-
  ing in the creek, enjoying two family weddings, going to a fair,
  joining in hymn sings with other Mennonite youth, and helping
  prepare for school to begin anew.
  ISBN 978-0-7369-6090-8 (pbk.)
  ISBN 978-0-7369-6091-5 (eBook)
  [1. Farm life—Fiction. 2. Summer—Fiction. 3. Family life—Fic-
  tion. 4. Mennonites—Fiction.] I. Title.
  PZ7.H95687Sum 2014
  [Fic]—dc23
                                                    2013047728

Printed in the United States of America

  14 15 16 17 18 19 20 21 / VP-JH / 10 9 8 7 6 5 4 3 2 1

Thank you to my siblings for all the help recalling summertime memories.

Contents

These true stories recall my happy
childhood days growing up in a large,
loving Mennonite family. We lived in
Lancaster County, Pennsylvania, in a
community made up of many Amish and
other Mennonite families who shared
the big and small events of our lives.

Chapter One

The Rhythm of Summer

I settled into summertime with its rhythm of daily chores. In the morning and evening, I helped Dad milk our fifty dairy cows. During the day I helped Mom with the meals and other housekeeping chores. Occasionally the whole family helped with the fieldwork.

As the warm temperatures rose, so did my hopes for the first swim of the summer season.

The stream that flowed through our farm was called "Middle Creek." Dad said it had lots of springs flowing into it, so the water stayed cold longer than other creeks in the area.

The day we helped Mom harvest the green beans from the garden was hot. As sister Ruth and Mom picked bucket after bucket of beans, sister Eva Mae and I snipped off the ends. Mom then steamed the vegetables in hot water, and after they cooled, my youngest brother, Aaron Ray, helped pack them in bags for the freezer. Eva Mae suggested we test the water for swimming after finishing the beans. With a plan like that, our job suddenly seemed to go faster.

I glanced out the window just in time to see the neighbor boys riding their bikes past our place. With towels and inflated inner tubes draped over their shoulders, it was obvious they were going swimming too. How could they have known about our intentions? Once again they had interfered with our plans!

That family lived to the south of our farm and across the creek. They were a large family. Seven of the eight children were boys. We got along—most of the time.

Just recently my brothers and sisters and I had cleared a path through the play woods in our neighborhood in hopes of secretly building a hut. The neighbor boys found the new path, and with a can of blue spray paint, they painted the words "NO GIRLS ALLOWED" on the rock by the entrance.

Spitefully we sprayed "NO BOYS AL-LOWED" over their message in another color. All week the tension built as we battled back and forth and sprayed messages on the rock. It wasn't long before the rock was removed, and we felt a little guilty. All seemed fine when on Sunday afternoon, the neighbor boys kindly invited us to play a game of baseball in their big front yard.

We played inning after inning and cheered

each other on. Afterward their mom treated us with cookies and cold lemonade. As we ate, we talked about the good game we had played, and there was no mention about the play-woods war.

Since we were not allowed to swim with the boys, we would have to wait until they finished. "There they go again, messing up our plans," I moaned.

My sister grinned and said, "Don't worry. This way they will scare away the snakes and snapping turtles for us."

"Good idea," I said. I felt better as I turned to finish the last bucket of beans. During kitchen cleanup, we noticed the boys returning from their swim. *So soon?* I wondered. Perhaps the water was still too cold for swimming, but we decided to try it for ourselves.

Soon Ruth, Eva Mae, and I ducked under the pasture fence and followed the cow path along the creek to the far end of the pasture where there was an area in the creek deep enough for swimming. We called this area the "swimming hole." Eagerly I scampered down the bank to the water's edge and tested the water with my toes. "Oh!" I cried, surprised by the chill and quickly pulling my toes out of the water.

Next to the swimming hole was a huge sycamore tree with a large hollow trunk—large enough for us to go inside—and thick curving branches reaching out above the water. Our swinging rope dangled from one of those big branches.

After stepping inside the trunk to hang up my towel, I looked around the area. The neighbor boys had begun repairing the small dam at the mouth of the swimming hole. We decided to continue their cleanup efforts. Spring floods and wandering cows had disturbed the dam, so we hunted for rocks on the creek bank and added them to the dam, leaving a small opening to create a swifter current. We then floated on our backs and let the current carry us downstream. Knee deep in water, we hunted for more large rocks on the creek bottom until we were wet and shivering.

Ruthie looked at me and said, "Your lips are blue!"

I looked back at her and replied, "Yours are blue too!" We wrapped ourselves in our large bath towels and headed barefoot back to the house.

Late that afternoon my two oldest sisters, Vera and Alta, had returned from their day's work at the sewing factory in town. They were very close in age, only fourteen months apart, and they shared the same car to drive to and from their jobs.

After changing into dry clothes, I felt cooled and very refreshed by the swim and a bit hungry, so I stepped into the kitchen for a little snack. Vera and Alta were there having a very intense discussion with Mom and Dad. I quickly retreated and leaned on the door frame to listen. It seemed both of their boyfriends had proposed marriage around the same time. Since it was tradition for weddings to be held at the home of the bride, they were fussing and fuming about who would marry first. My Dad had concerns about a wedding being held during the summertime, an especially hot and busy time of the year. He sat straddling a kitchen chair with his arms crossed over the backrest.

"How about a double wedding?" Mom suggested.

"No," Dad said. "That wouldn't work. There is not enough room in this house for so many guests."

Finally they agreed that both of my sisters would marry—but several weeks apart.

I returned to my bedroom to absorb the news. My sisters were getting married, and we were having two weddings in one summer!

Chapter Two

Preparation

Immediately the work pace picked up around the farm. Along with daily chores, we worked on extra projects. After their day's work, my teen brothers, Earl and Marvin, helped too.

Dad repainted the trim on the house. Mom planted extra flowers along the edge of the vegetable garden and around the house. She even planted some in front of the milk house by the barn. She canned lots of garden vegetables and fruit—including a hundred quarts of peaches!—that summer, some for our family and some for my sisters' new homes. Alta was busy sewing her wedding dress and, from another fabric, three matching dresses for us younger sisters.

By twilight we were exhausted and often retreated to the back porch. On most nights we didn't talk much. We would sit quietly, listening to the late evening sounds of crickets and birds joining the music from the nearby creek gurgling and flowing around rocks and logs. Occasionally, though, we enjoyed a summer's eve tradition—hymn singing with music from our family's accordion. On one special night, our neighbor Martha, from the farm across the creek, stepped out onto her back porch with her harmonica and joined in the music. As the soft light of the rising moon lit the meadow, we sang song after song.

"Far away beyond the starlit skies, where the love-light never, never dies…"

"Will the circle be unbroken, by and by, Lord, by and by? In a better home awaiting in the sky…"

We sang songs we had learned from Mom or at school, and somehow I knew I would miss times like this—singing with all my sisters—when I was all grown up. I hoped we would carry on the tradition.

Early in the morning, Vera and Alta woke to the sound of fluttering wings in their shared bedroom. Our old, eighteenth-century farmhouse had a problem with bats in the attic, and whenever the person who cleaned the attic forgot to stuff the rags back beneath the door leading to the upstairs hallway, the bats got into the house. It was always frightening to hear the bats flying around the bedroom. We would duck under the covers and holler for Mom. She would come rushing in with a broom and a bucket of water. With the broom she would whack the bat into the bucket of water and rush it out of the house.

This time when Alta called for Mom, Mom hollered right back from the other side of the bedroom door, "You are getting married. You are old enough to get rid of your own bats!"

My sisters looked at each other and then at the bat. "You do it!" Alta told Vera.

"No!" Vera answered. "I can't. I need to get ready for work." While one tried to push the job on to the other, the bat found a landing place on Alta's neatly ironed wedding dress.

Infuriated, Alta leaped out of bed and wacked the bat herself.

Now Alta was ready for marriage.

Near the end of the week, we loaded the house furniture onto the hay wagons and stored it away in the barn. We set up rows and rows of folding chairs in four adjacent rooms on the first floor of our house until it began to look like a church.

On Friday evening, several neighbors arrived to help with last-minute preparations. Fannie, Ida, and Ella gathered around a sack of potatoes all evening. They laughed and visited with each other as they peeled potatoes into five-gallon buckets filled with water. This kept the potatoes fresh until they could be cooked the next day. Other ladies sliced cheese, cut the ham, dished relish, and served up strawberry preserves. In the back shanty, I gazed at the rows of sheet cakes that filled the long table. Each piece had a tiny icing rosebud with fancy white trim around it. I could hardly wait for Saturday to see how wedding cake tasted!

Chapter Three

A Wedding at Home

On the morning of the wedding, we finished barn chores extra early. After changing into my new dress, which was made just for the wedding, I looked for a matching handkerchief. Even though I had already decided that I was not going to cry, I went downstairs to the dresser where Mom kept the Sunday handkerchiefs—just in case. The dresser wasn't in its usual spot. It was stored away in the barn with the rest of the furniture. I ran to the barn, hurriedly climbed onto the wagon, and ducked under the blankets. I reached through the maze of household furniture and was barely able to open the small top drawer of the dresser. Squeezing my hand into the small opening, I found a blue and white handkerchief.

Outside I heard the sound of guests beginning to arrive. Some came by horse and buggy, others by car. Our family now belonged to a Mennonite church that allowed for black cars. Since other colors were considered worldly, the cars had to be painted black all over. Most of my relatives remained in the horse-and-buggy church.

I stood in the yard and watched the friends of the bride and groom, whom we called "hostlers." They served the guests by meeting them as they drove up to the door. As the guests walked to the house, the hostlers took the horse, unhitched it from the buggy, marked the harness and buggy with a number in chalk, parked the buggy, and led the horse to the barnyard. There they tied the horse to a hay wagon with the other horses. When guests arrived in a car, the hostlers parked the car with the other cars in long rows along the edge of the pasture. For this service the hostlers expected a tip. I had heard at my cousin's wedding that when the hostlers didn't get a tip, they played tricks on the guests by mixing up the harnesses and hitching up the horses to the wrong buggy.

It was a warm and sticky August day, and the house seemed to grow hotter as it filled with all one hundred and twenty guests. I took my seat near the front row with my family. The minister stood in the east doorway so guests could hear him in every room. He opened the service with a traditional wedding song, which also served as the processional. Together the guests quietly sang,

> Tread softly, tread softly,
> the Master is here.
> Tread softly, tread softly,
> He bids us draw near.

As we sang, I could hear the footsteps of the bridal party coming down the stairs. They made their way carefully through the narrow aisles and between the rows of tightly packed chairs. Beside the bride and groom, only two couples served as attendants. We called them "nevasitza." The song continued as they took their seats in front of the minister. My sister looked nervous but happy in her new, pale blue wedding dress. The dark suit her boyfriend, Ed, wore was already wet with sweat. Several ministers took turns preaching the two-hour service.

I could hear the clatter of kettles and dishes coming from the kitchen as the aunts and uncles prepared dinner. A delicious smell of cooking food filled the house, and I imagined the flurry of activity in the kitchen. In my mind I pictured the cakes on the back shanty table.

The minister preached on and on, and sweat trickled down my back. Thunder rumbled in the distance. The minister must have heard the thunder too, because he cut the sermon a little short and sat down. When the bishop stood up, the room grew very quiet as the bride and groom rose and stood in front of him. He gave them marriage instructions from the Bible, and then he led them through the marriage vows.

He turned to Ed first and said, "I ask you as groom, do you promise to take our sister in the faith, Alta, as thy wife to love her and stand by her in sickness or in sorrow or what-soever the Lord may cause to come upon her, and take upon you the weightier matters of life and to provide for her, and to live a peace-able and Christian life with her, and not to forsake her as long as God grants you life?"

Ed answered with yes, and then the bishop turned to Alta and asked her a similar ques-tion. "Yes," she softly answered. Tears came to my eyes as I listened.

The bishop knelt with the couple to pray. Clasping his hands over their adjoined hands, he said, "The God of Abraham, the God of Isaac, and the God of Jacob go with you and help you go forth as husband and wife. Fear God and keep his commandments, whereunto I wish you the peace and blessings of God. Amen."

After the prayer he rose, and the guests sang the words of a closing hymn.

> He leadeth me, He leadeth me,
> By his own hand He leadeth me...

The newlyweds exited the room first, and then our family followed. As the guests sang, they followed us outside to the front yard. In the shade of our tall pine tree, guests congratulated the bride and groom and shook their hands. I watched the long row of people file past to celebrate with my family. It was hard to believe my sister Alta and her boyfriend were suddenly husband and wife.

Chapter Four

Wedding Crumbs

While guests visited in the front yard, the waitresses and hostlers hurried to set up tables in the rooms where the service was held. More thunder rumbled in the west, and we all hoped the storm would hold off until everyone was safe inside.

Soon a loud voice was heard from across the yard. The couples were called by name and invited to the house to be seated at the tables inside. I was glad my family got to eat first along with the bridal party. After the minister said a prayer of thanks, waitresses passed steaming bowls brimming with mashed potatoes, brown buttered noodles, ham and gravy, peas, chow chow relish, and cheese.

For dessert we had fruit salad and the special strawberry dessert Mom had canned earlier in the summer just for the wedding. It looked as delicious as ever with whipped cream piled high on top. Finally a waitress put a piece of wedding cake on my plate. It was much softer and sweeter than our everyday homemade cakes. I wanted to eat it slowly, but we had to hurry away from the table to make room for the next group of guests to eat. The waitresses moved quickly to stack and carry the dishes to the kitchen. There they hastily washed the dishes and reset the tables. The waitresses would have to do this two more times before all the guests were served.

I followed some guests upstairs to my sister's bedroom where the gift receivers had placed the gifts the guests had brought for the couple. The gifts were unwrapped, recorded in a guest book so that the bride and groom would know who had given which gift, and piled high on the bed, dresser, and cedar chest. We looked at all those things my sister would need to begin housekeeping. Nearby was a basket of small pieces of wedding fabric samples. Each girlfriend took a piece of fabric for their scrapbooks.

In the midst of the chatter of visiting friends, I noticed a commotion in the back of the bedroom. Ed and Alta had spied the whisperings of the girlfriends in the bedroom. The bride and groom, knowing what their friends were planning, fled through the house. Hand in hand, they ran down the back stairs. Their friends ran after them in hot pursuit. It was tradition from the past for girlfriends of the bride to grab her and lift her upside down to "shake the girlhood from her." Likewise, the groom was thrown over the barnyard fence by his friends to "remove him from his boyhood."

Ed and Alta ran past the cooks and out the back of the house, determined to escape the ritual. They ducked into the garage of the old house on our property where Ed had carefully hidden his neatly polished black, brand-new 1973 Plymouth Road Runner. Ed's father had given him that car in exchange for working on the farm. Safely inside, they were shocked to discover what had been done to their car. Outside, a laughing crowd gathered as Ed slowly backed the car from the garage. In secret, Alta's English coworkers from the sewing factory found the hidden car, filled it with bits of crepe paper, hung streamers from the doors and windows, and strung empty tin cans from the bumper. The surprise was complete with a "JUST MARRIED!" sign in the back window.

The cans clanged and rattled noisily as Ed slowly drove down the road. He tooted the horn as they started their wedding trip out West, and we laughed and waved goodbye. The storm that had threatened all afternoon arrived just as the last of the buggies and cars started for home.

In the house, the cooks were finishing the cleanup, and Dad was in a jolly mood. He was relieved the storm had held off, and all had gone as planned. He jokingly teased his brothers as they washed the last of the kettles and dishes. *Woe sin die Hochzich brockle?* "Where are the wedding crumbs?" he called to the cooks. Dad had already milked the cows, and with barn chores finished, he was ready to enjoy the leftovers. The kitchen table was loaded with dishes of leftover food from the wedding dinner. I went straight for a piece of pretty wedding cake.

From across the table, I noticed Dad's face. Something was wrong. He didn't look well. Fear gripped my heart as Dad struggled to breathe. He stumbled toward the door. My brothers guided my dad outside. I followed not far behind, clasping my hands to my chest as I prayed, "God, please help my dad."

Dad was having trouble using his new false teeth and choking on a piece of ham. His face was turning blue as he struggled for air. Ruthie ran back to the house and started to dial nine-one-one for an ambulance. Just then someone from the crowd gathered around Dad shouted, "He's got it out!" and Ruthie stopped dialing for the ambulance.

"Oh, thank you, Lord," I prayed as I released

the breath I had been holding. Gratefully we all returned to enjoy what Dad called the "wedding crumbs." As we ate, the adults talked about the wedding. I was glad to think that, in a few weeks, we would get to do this all over again at my sister Vera's wedding!

Chapter Five

Rough and Tumble

Our lives settled back into a normal routine, at least for a short time. Late one morning, Dad announced that it was "Rough and Tumble" time. Near the end of August each summer, Dad took us to a local thresherman's reunion called "Rough and Tumble." This was our only yearly getaway.

Aaron Ray got in the front seat of the car with Dad. Eva Mae, Ruthie, and I climbed into the backseat. Dad whistled an old folk song as we drove down Route 30 and talked about farming days when he was a boy. He told us again how the old steam engine came to his family's farm to thresh wheat for the harvest. As we approached the fair grounds, I could see smoke from the engines in the distance. Soon I heard the exciting sound of their whistles.

At the entrance, Dad pulled out his billfold and handed each of us girls a five-dollar bill. "Here you go. Get yourself something to eat," he said.

I stared at the money in my hand. Never before had Dad given us money to spend as we pleased!

"Aaron Ray will go with me," he continued. "You girls are old enough to be on your own. Meet me at the exit at four o'clock."

At first it was a little scary to be on our own, so we girls decided to stay together. I folded the money carefully and placed it in the pocket of my dress. To keep it safe, I kept my hand over it inside my pocket. We began to walk around the grounds, starting in the direction of the trains and visiting displays on the way.

First we stopped to watch an old lady, who

was dressed in a long apron, stir apple butter in an old iron kettle over an open fire. We listened as she described the process of making apple butter in the old days. When she offered us each a sample on small crackers, we eagerly accepted. It was sweet and spicy. We made our apple butter spread at home by mixing applesauce, sugar, and spices in a large roasting pan, and then slowly cooking it in the oven. We had to stir it often over several hours. This apple butter, which had been cooked over an open fire, tasted extra special.

Next we watched a man wearing a straw hat make homemade brooms from straw. We walked on, continuing past the sawmill and

a noisy old engine that powered the belt of a big saw blade. Beneath the noise of the engine emerged a sweet melody of a nearby steam-powered pipe organ.

I was drawn by the music. I wanted to stay

and listen, but my sisters were eager to move on. At the food tent, we each bought a hamburger and shared a large order of French fries. For us French fries were a rare treat that tasted extra special with ketchup drizzled all over them.

I had trouble drinking the soda that came with the meal. Somehow it stung my nose and throat every time I took a swallow. I decided I liked fresh-squeezed, homemade lemonade much better.

For dessert we watched homemade ice cream being churned by a one-cylinder hit-and-miss engine. At home we churned our ice cream by hand, but this ice cream was made by the barrel! When it was finished, we were allowed to purchase a small dish filled with creamy vanilla ice cream. We ate it slowly as we continued our walk. Eventually we found the train and purchased a ticket.

When the conductor shouted loudly, "All aboard!" we climbed onto the seat of the open car.

Slowly the engine pulled the train away from the station, blowing smoke and hissing steam noisily. I loved the sound of the long whistle blowing as the train circled the outskirts of the fairgrounds.

I looked for Dad in the crowd of people. When the train passed the wheat field, I spotted him standing with a group of men watching an old black steam engine running a threshing machine. His straw hat was in his hand, and on his head he wore a blue and white engineer's cap. Aaron Ray stood beside him with a smaller matching cap on his head.

Too soon the train pulled back into the station. The conductor opened the exit door, we climbed down, and walked to a nearby grove of trees where musicians had gathered to play their banjos, fiddles, and other stringed instruments. I was fascinated by how well they played together. Soon someone joined the group with a harmonica. They sang and played "Oh! Susanna" and "Oh, Dem Golden Slippers."

My sisters agreed to sit with me a little while to listen. I tapped my toes to the rhythm of

"Cripple Creek." Then the music slowed down as the musicians played "Home on the Range." I knew that song well and quietly sang along. I watched and wished I could play a stringed instrument.

"Come on," Ruthie urged. "We'd better start heading back." We didn't have a watch with us, so we guessed by the position of the sun that it was late afternoon and soon time to meet Dad.

We passed a few more displays along the way and paused to watch a man cut shingles with a small steam engine. He then branded the board with a picture of an old engine with smoke billowing from its smokestack. Across the top he engraved the words "Rough and Tumble 1979." We decided to buy one and hang it in our bedroom. Since the three of us shared the same bedroom, we could share the souvenir.

We waited for Dad at the exit but not for long. Dad was in a hurry to get home for the evening milking. On our ride home in the warm late afternoon, we drove with the windows rolled down. As the wind blew in my face and through the wisps of hair around my braids, I thought on all the special things I had seen that afternoon. The whistle of the engines lingered in my ears. I looked down at the shingle in my lap and ran my fingers across the engraving. The souvenir would help me remember this special summer vacation visit to Rough and Tumble.

Chapter Six

Summer's End

During the last week of August, just a few days before school began, several local families met after morning chores at our private one-room school to prepare the schoolhouse and the playground for another school year.

Two men climbed up on the roof to fix the old iron bell while others cleaned up the outhouse. The neighbor next to the school had kept his horse in the fenced-in playground during the summer to graze so that the grass stayed low. Now the horse was led back to his own pasture, the manure was cleaned up, and the grass was neatly trimmed with a mower.

The women washed the windows, desks, and floors of the school, and we children helped as much as we could by dusting off the schoolbooks and hymnbooks. Then we played on the swing set and seesaws on the playground. With everyone working together, the job was easily finished by noon.

Mom and Dad went home in the pickup truck, but I decided to walk the quarter mile home to our farm. I walked slowly down the road from the schoolhouse, turned right, and then took a shortcut through the hay field. I found the trail that led to the woods by the creek.

I didn't want summer vacation to end. I stopped on the creek bank to watch an early fallen leaf float along the current. A dragonfly buzzed nearby. There were so many exciting things about summer to remember—my sisters' weddings, the fun at the swimming hole, and our visit to Rough and Tumble.

I continued the walk through the woods and past the hut we had tried to build. The walls leaned to the left, and the roof sagged dangerously in the middle. I passed the remains of the neighbor boys' hut and saw that theirs had already collapsed. As I exited the woods, I pulled my thoughts away from summertime and suddenly remembered the invitation our family had received to the Hoovers' annual watermelon party. The Hoovers were neighbors who sold watermelon and other produce at a small roadside stand. They shared their harvests with the neighborhood by hosting a watermelon party and hymn sing at summer's end. The invitation said to bring our hymnbooks and lawn chairs. I ran the rest of the way home.

During milking time Friday evening, I could hear horses and buggies trot past our farm to the Hoovers' place nearby. Some passed on bicycles, and others walked and pulled their younger children along in wagons. My sisters and I decided to walk there too. As we approached the Hoovers' farm, I could see a crowd already gathered under the shade of the large maple tree in the yard. The men hung their hats on tree limbs or on the backs of chairs and fence posts. Neighbors sat together in a circle, sharing hymnbooks, and began the singing.

I always enjoy a chance to sing with others, but it was extra special to sing with such a large crowd. The women's alto and soprano voices blended beautifully with the men's tenor and bass voices.

Many of my classmates were there too. I was happy to see them again. We sang together with the adults as the evening sun began to set across the fields in the west.

Long tables were lined up by the shed and loaded with cut-up pieces of watermelon. Another table had drinks, whoopie pies, and an assortment of yummy looking homemade baked goods. Before long I heard whisperings among the girls that the teenagers were playing games at a neighboring farm. We left the circle of singers, helped ourselves to a few cookies, and headed out across the backyard.

We tried to sneak quietly between the rows of tall cornstalks in the field. Before long we could hear sounds of accordion music coming from the open barn doors. We slowly approached the party and sat in the grass near the entrance to watch.

The Old Order Mennonites called these games "stomping," which was not considered a worldly dance. They twirled their partners around and stepped in time with the tune of old folk songs.

A small light flickered from a lantern hanging from the barn door, casting enough light for the dancers to see. Neighbor Suzie saw us watching and motioned for us to come and join them. Before the next song started, she briefly showed us a few steps to a simple dance. I felt too shy to dance with the boys, so I partnered with the girls in my class. We played until we were hot and tired out.

It was dark by the time we headed back through the cornfield. The rows were thirty inches apart, just right for a trail through the corn. Normally I wasn't afraid of cornfields, but now that it was dark and spooky, we stayed close together and brushed aside the cornstalks with upraised arms. We ran out at the other side of the field and headed straight for the cold drinks and sweet, cool water-melon. We gathered in a circle as we ate and talked about school starting on Monday.

The younger children played tag in the yard as our parents stood around visiting with each other. Soon families started leaving the barn-yard in their buggies for the trip home. We walked the half mile home on the moon-lit road while the smell of late summer crops filled the night air.

When we crossed over the bridge, I could

see the lights of home. Having seen my classmates that evening, I felt I was now ready for
school to begin after all.

Glossary

Old Order Mennonite

a branch of the Mennonite church whose lifestyle is similar to the Amish in tradition and transportation (using horse and buggy instead of a vehicle)

swimming hole

a deep spot in a creek or stream where children can swim or wade

tradition

beliefs and customs handed down from parents to children through many years

attendants

like bridesmaids and groomsmen, those who stand with the bride and groom during the wedding and take care of the couple's wedding details

hostlers

friends of the bride and groom who serve by taking care of the wedding guests' horses and buggies and are tipped for their service (If not tipped, a hostler might play tricks on you!)

handkerchief

a small square of cotton or linen, which is usually embroidered or trimmed with lace, carried in a pocket, and used to blow one's nose or wipe away tears

whoopies

short for whoopee pie, a common dessert in Lancaster County, which is made from two soft (usually chocolate) cookies with a creamy icing or filling sandwiched between

stomping

an Old Order Mennonite game that's kind of like a barn dance, which was not considered worldly and, thus, not forbidden

Wedding Jam

1 quart fresh or frozen strawberries
    (or any other kind of fruit)
2 cups water
¼ cup granulated sugar (more or less to taste)
2 tablespoons clear jel (regular, not instant),
    dissolved in ⅓ cup water

Cook strawberries in 2 cups water until soft. Add sugar and bring back to a boil slowly. Stir in the dissolved clear jel and bring back to a boil again. Cook a few more minutes until thick. Remove from heat and cool completely. Serve with Real Whipped Cream (recipe follows).

You may can the jam like Mother did for the wedding by pouring the hot, thickened jam into canning jars, sealing each jar with a lid, and boiling the jars in a canner for ten minutes.

Real Whipped Cream

½ cup heavy cream
pinch of sugar
¼ teaspoon vanilla

In a small mixing bowl, whip the cream using a mixer until thick. Blend in sugar and vanilla. Enjoy!

the newlyweds
and their gifts

Elva (on the left with
pigtails and rolled-down
socks) with her sisters on the
day of the wedding

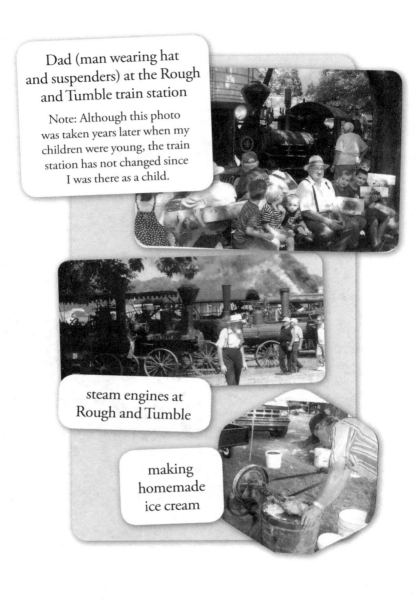

Dad (man wearing hat and suspenders) at the Rough and Tumble train station

Note: Although this photo was taken years later when my children were young, the train station has not changed since I was there as a child.

steam engines at Rough and Tumble

making homemade ice cream

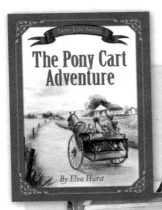

Also written and illustrated
by Elva Hurst
Pony Cart Adventure

To visit Elva's Barnyard Art Gallery online,
go to **www.elvaschalkart.com**.

You can also write to

Barnyard Art
1519 Brunnerville Road
Lititz, Pennsylvania 17543